GOLDEN EAGLES

A SOLO JOURNEY

REBECCA HIRSCH
AND MARIA KORAN

www.av2books.com

MEDIA ENHANCED BOOKS
AV²
BY WEIGL™
ADDED VALUE • AUDIO VISUAL

AV² provides enriched content that supplements and complements this book. Weigl's AV² books strive to create inspired learning and engage young minds in a total learning experience.

Your AV² Media Enhanced books come alive with...

Audio
Listen to sections of the book read aloud.

Key Words
Study vocabulary, and complete a matching word activity.

Go to www.av2books.com, and enter this book's unique code.

Video
Watch informative video clips.

Quizzes
Test your knowledge.

BOOK CODE
F834359

Embedded Weblinks
Gain additional information for research.

Slide Show
View images and captions, and prepare a presentation.

AV² **by Weigl** brings you media enhanced books that support active learning.

Try This!
Complete activities and hands-on experiments.

... and much, much more!

Published by AV² by Weigl
350 5ᵗʰ Avenue, 59ᵗʰ Floor
New York, NY 10118
Website: www.av2books.com

Library of Congress Cataloging-in-Publication Data

Names: Cosson, M. J., and Koran, Maria.
Title: Golden eagles : a solo journey / M.J. Cosson and Maria Koran.
Description: New York, NY : AV2 by Weigl, [2017] | Series: Nature's great journeys | Includes bibliographical references and index.
Identifiers: LCCN 2016004421 (print) | LCCN 2016011668 (ebook) | ISBN 9781489645159 (hard cover : alk. paper) | ISBN 9781489649911 (soft cover : alk. paper) | ISBN 9781489645166 (Multi-user ebk.)
Subjects: LCSH: Golden eagles--Migration--Juvenile literature. | Golden eagle--Juvenile literature. | Animal migration--Juvenile literature.
Classification: LCC QL696.F32 C685 2017 (print) | LCC QL696.F32 (ebook) | DDC 598.9/423--dc23
LC record available at http://lccn.loc.gov/2016004421

Printed in the United States of America in Brainerd, Minnesota
1 2 3 4 5 6 7 8 9 0 20 19 18 17 16

072016
071416

Project Coordinator: Maria Koran   Art Director: Terry Paulhus

Contents

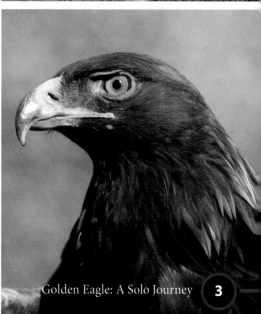

GOLDEN EAGLES

Golden eagles in flight are a wonder to see. They **soar** high with their long wings. They also swoop low to catch **prey**. Many golden eagles migrate in the fall. They fly south in search of warmer weather. That is where they can find more prey. In the spring, those same golden eagles migrate north to have babies. Golden eagles do not migrate in a flocks like geese. Golden eagles migrate alone.

The golden eagle's lifetime journey is its migration. This is when an animal moves from one **habitat** to another. Migrations happen for many reasons. Some animals move to be in warmer weather where there is more food. There they can reproduce or have their babies. And these migrations can be short distances, such as from a mountaintop to its valley. Or they can be long distances, like the golden eagle's journey.

Golden eagles have strong wings for flying.

MIGRATION MAP

Golden eagles live in Europe, Asia, North Africa, and North America. Not all golden eagles migrate. Some live all year in places where winters are not too cold. Many eagles born in Alaska and Canada migrate south. Some fly as far south as Mexico. Golden eagles have a **latitudinal** migration.

Golden eagles from Alaska and western Canada fly south through the Rocky Mountains. They winter in the southwestern United States and Mexico. Golden eagles from eastern Canada fly south along the Appalachian Mountains. They fly through the states of New York and Pennsylvania. They spend the winter in Virginia and other southern states. A smaller number of golden eagles fly toward the Midwest.

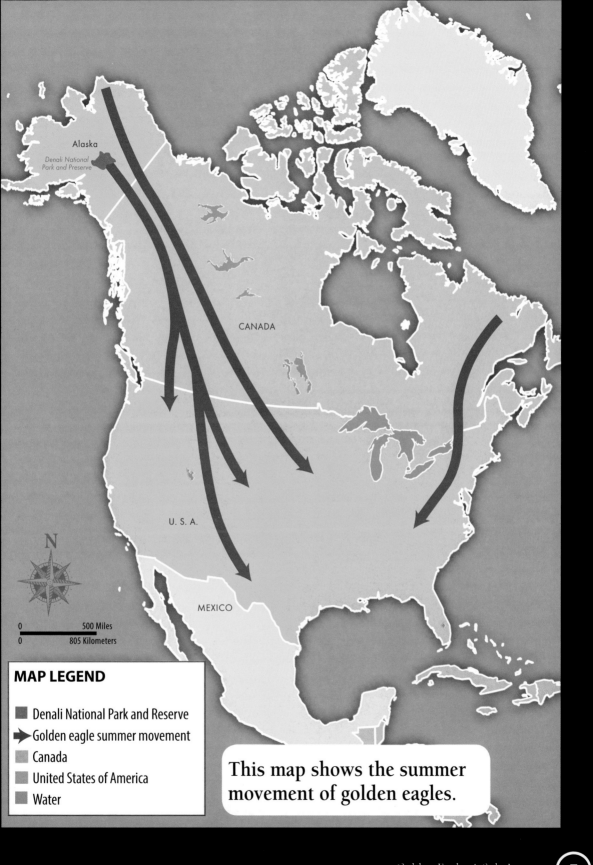

Alaska

Denali National
Park and Preserve

CANADA

U. S. A.

MEXICO

N

0   500 Miles
0   805 Kilometers

MAP LEGEND

Denali National Park and Reserve
Golden eagle summer movement
Canada
United States of America
Water

This map shows the summer movement of golden eagles.

The golden eagle is North America's largest bird of prey.

PROUD BIRDS

Golden eagles are proud-looking birds. They have dark brown feathers topped by some gold feathers. The gold is mostly on their heads and necks. These eagles can be more than 3 feet (1 m) tall. They weigh between 8 and 15 pounds (4 and 7 kg). They can have a **wingspan** of more than 7 feet (2 m). Males and females look alike, but females are bigger.

The golden eagle is the national bird of Mexico.

MAKING A NEST

Denali National Park is in Alaska. Many golden eagles **breed** in this northern area. These breeding grounds need to have certain things. The eagles need rocky cliffs on which to build nests. They need open land with big trees. They need high spots to watch for prey. And high nests keep their babies safe from **predators**.

Most eagles return north by April. This is the time when golden eagles choose a mate and build a nest. Golden eagles keep the same mate for life. The mates find a **territory**. They stay in their own territories to hunt and raise their young. They do not mark their territories. But they fly along its edges. They will fight other eagles that try to enter their territories.

Golden eagle pairs work together to build nests of sticks. The nests are called **aeries**. The eagles line their aeries with soft moss or grass. They often return to old aeries, too. They fix them up for the nesting season. They make their aeries bigger and better. Some eagles keep several aeries. When an aerie is done, it is time to lay eggs.

Golden eagles mate for life.

The golden eagle is a booted eagle. It is called that because feathers cover its legs.

Chicks hatch
in May or June.

LIFE IN THE SUMMER

Female golden eagles lay from one to four eggs. But most nests have two eggs. Some eggs are white and some have brown spots. Females spend the most time sitting on the eggs. But males help, too. They keep the eggs safe and warm.

Chicks **hatch** from March through June. Females take care of their young in the first weeks. The males hunt for food for their families. Later parents take turns feeding their young small pieces of meat.

Parents spend most of the summer hunting. They are too busy to teach their young how to fly and hunt. The chicks become **fledglings** as they grow. The fledglings must eat a lot. They need to build up fat in their bodies. That fat will keep them going when they cannot find food.

Fledglings spend the summer getting ready to leave the nest.

When they are about 60 to 70 days old, the fledglings are ready to fly. They teach themselves to fly. They practice all summer. They stay close by their aeries. They build their muscles. They need to be strong for their fall migrations. And they need to start hunting for their own food.

By the end of summer the fledglings are bigger and stronger. The brown fledglings have a white patch on their tails. They have white under their wings. At four months they can leave their parents. The eagles that migrate can begin their long trip south.

This young eagle will have its adult feathers in three years.

FLYING SOUTH

In late September or early October, the fledglings are ready to be on their own. Fledglings that stay in their area are ready to hunt for prey. Fledglings that fly south begin to migrate. Some older eagles stay in the north through winter. There will be more prey for those who stay. Others wait before heading south. The young eagles have a head start. The eagles do not all leave at the same time. They fly alone and go different ways. And each eagle might not fly the same route twice.

Golden eagles use the mountains to help them fly. The eagles seek cliff lines and ridges that lie north to south. They fly during the middle of the day. It is hottest then. The heated winds cause a **thermal** wind along the cliffs. Heat from open land can also make thermals. A thermal wind is heated air in cooler air. The heated air rises above the cooler air. The eagles catch the thermal winds. They ride the winds with their wings spread. They save their energy. They rarely flap their wings.

The fledglings do not always fly high. They sometimes fly low and hunt prey. Golden eagles eat rabbits and squirrels. They also eat birds, foxes, cats, and lizards. Their eyes can see very well. Golden eagles can spot a rabbit from up to 2 miles (3 km) away. They can dive at high speeds to catch the rabbit.

If they cannot find live food, golden eagles will eat **carrion**. Sometimes they cannot find anything to eat. Then they live off fat stored in their bodies. Golden eagles can live off their own fat for several days. Many birds are too small to rely on stored fat.

The young eagles take four to nine weeks to migrate south. They usually make one or two rest stops of a few days on their way. They also stop to sleep and to hunt and eat prey. Older eagles take less time. Golden eagles fly between 500 to 3,000 miles (805 to 5,000 km) as they migrate south.

Eagles begin to migrate in the fall.

FINDING THEIR WAY

How do fledgling golden eagles find their way? On their own, they know to head south. They know how to use thermals to save energy. They know how to hunt prey. They know to eat carrion when they cannot find other food. Some scientists think the **knowledge** is in the golden eagle's **genes**. They do not need to learn it.

How do the eagles know where to stop for the winter? Scientists think golden eagles stop when they find enough food. They might stop at a cliff or tall tree on a plain. Or they find a power or telephone pole. When their store of fat runs out, they will stop for the winter. Or migrating golden eagles might stop for the winter when they reach open territory. If no other eagles are there, an eagle will take the territory.

Eagles find prey to eat as they migrate.

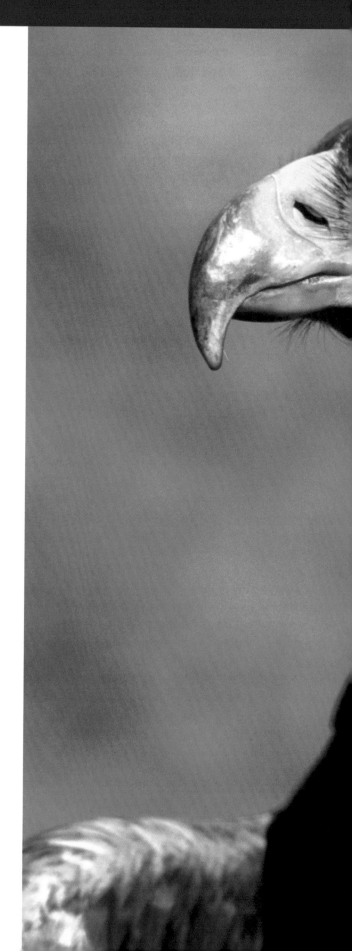

WINTER HOMES

The golden eagle **population** in Colorado and other western states grows in the winter. Golden eagles are found in Colorado because many live there year round. They can be seen on plains. They are in mountain valleys. They perch on cliffs.

Golden eagles avoid people and cities. They do not winter on mountaintops because there is very little food there. But many golden eagles spend summers on mountaintops. They migrate down the mountain in the winter in search of food.

Golden eagles are found in Colorado.

Golden eagles and other birds of prey have a third eyelid called a nictitating membrane.

Golden eagles may have migration knowledge in their genes.

FLYING BACK NORTH

Golden eagles head north between March and mid-June. It takes about the same amount of time for older golden eagles to migrate north as it did to go south. The fledglings that left Alaska and Canada in the fall will return in the spring. They will not return home, though. They are too young for the breeding grounds.

Golden eagles have long lives for birds. In the wild they live to be 20 years or older. Golden eagles start their own families when they are about four to five years old. For the first few years, they return near to the area where they were born in the summers. Young eagles that were born in Denali National Park in Alaska will not return to the park. But they will return to Alaska for the summers until they are old enough to breed.

Young golden eagles take less time to fly north in the spring than they did to fly south in the fall. These young eagles are older and more experienced at migration. They became better flyers over the winter.

Many golden eagles return to Alaska in the summer.

THREATS TO THE EAGLES

In the past there were no laws to stop golden eagles from being hunted. Farmers and ranchers thought eagles harmed their animals. A farmer or rancher would kill an eagle. We now know that golden eagles do little harm to farm animals. Native Americans also hunted eagles. They use their feathers in **ceremonies**. The eagle feathers are very important for Native Americans.

Chemicals used in farming kill many eagles and other animals. Eagles eat animals that have died because of the farming chemicals. This can kill the eagles, too.

Golden eagles have lost much of their habitat because of people's actions. People now live where eagles once nested. They have raised large signs where eagles once perched. They have built roads where eagles once hunted. The wilds where golden eagles once lived and flew through now contain towers, windmills, and other tall buildings.

Windmills catch wind energy for people to use as power. Giant windmills dot the hills of many states. Wind turns the huge windmills. They make electricity. But the same wind also helps eagles on their migration. Many golden eagles die from flying into the windmills. Scientists are tracking the golden eagles' paths. They are trying to save the eagles. And they want to find safer places for the windmills.

Windmills are a threat to golden eagles' migration paths.

Golden eagles are at the top of their food chain. They have similar needs to many other animals. If people can save golden eagles in a certain habitat, they can help the other animals, too.

HELP FOR GOLDEN EAGLES

Today, people are trying to help golden eagles. It is against the law to harm eagles. It is also against the law to move or hurt their nests or eggs. Native Americans still use eagle feathers in their ceremonies. These include ceremonies for marriage, naming, and healing. The National Eagle Repository in Denver, Colorado, receives dead eagles. The repository is part of the government. It records information and keeps track of why the eagles died.

Members of Native American tribes are the only people who can have the dead eagles. They may only use the eagle's feathers for ceremonies. The feathers may not be sold. There is a list of about 5,000 Native Americans waiting for eagle feathers. It takes about three and a half years to receive a dead golden eagle.

Tracking helps scientists learn where golden eagles live and migrate.

Golden eagles need clear migration paths.

Scientists track eagles as they migrate. They catch the birds and put special instruments on them. The instruments send information to the scientists. They tell scientists where the eagles go. Scientists also use leg bands. The leg bands label the birds. **Satellites** also help track the eagles. This information is very important for the future of golden eagles. To save golden eagles, people need to learn where the birds go. People can then know where to avoid building.

To help golden eagles, people need know the problems that face the eagles. Then they can work to keep the eagles safe. Golden eagles need wind to help them migrate. They need the wilderness to hunt and raise their young. Scientists must continue to study the migration paths of golden eagles. Only by understanding where they go and what they do can we keep golden eagles from harm.

Researchers fit golden eagles with backpacks to carry satellite transmitters.

QUIZ

1 When are fledglings ready to be on their own?

A. In late September or early October

2 Why do eagles swoop low?

A. To catch prey

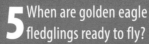

3 Are female golden eagles bigger or smaller than males?

A. Bigger

4 What are eagle nests called?

A. Aeries

5 When are golden eagle fledglings ready to fly?

A. At 60 to 70 days old

6 How do eagles fly without flapping their wings?

A. They ride on thermal winds.

7 How long do golden eagles live in the wild?

A. 20 years or longer

8 How many Native Americans are on the waiting list for feathers?

A. About 5,000

9 Name one breeding ground for golden eagles in Alaska.

A. Denali National Park

10 How do golden eagles carry satellite tracking transmitters?

A. With backpacks

KEY WORDS

aeries: Aeries are the large nests of birds of prey. Aeries are made bigger each year.

breed: To breed is to mate and produce young. Golden eagles breed during the spring and summer.

carrion: Carrion is a dead animal not killed by the animal eating it. Sometimes golden eagles eat carrion.

ceremonies: Ceremonies are formal actions, words, and music to celebrate an important event. Some Native Americans use golden eagle feathers in their ceremonies.

chemicals: Chemicals are materials made using chemistry. Farming chemicals can poison eagles.

fledglings: Fledglings are young birds just before and during when they are learning to fly. Chicks grow into fledglings.

genes: Genes are parts of the cells that have information about what young look like and how they act. Genes are found in all living things. Scientists think some knowledge can be passed to birds through their genes.

habitat: A habitat is a place that has the food, water, and shelter an animal needs to survive. Cliffs make a good habitat for golden eagles.

hatch: To hatch is to break out of an egg. Chicks hatch from their eggs.

knowledge: Knowledge is the things that an animal or person knows. An eagle may be born with certain knowledge.

latitudinal: Latitudinal relates to how far north and south something is from the equator. Golden eagles have a latitudinal migration.

population: A population is all the animals of one type that live in the same area. A golden eagle population lives in Colorado.

predators: Predators are animals that hunt and eat other animals. High nests keep predators away from young eagles.

prey: Prey is an animal that is hunted for food by another animal. Eagles hunt for prey.

satellites: Satellites are machines sent into space that move with the earth's orbit. Satellites can help scientists track golden eagles.

soar: To soar is to fly very high in the air. Golden eagles soar on thermal winds.

territory: A territory is the land that one animal marks for its own. Each golden eagle has its own territory.

thermal: A thermal is a rising current of warm air. Thermal winds help eagles save energy.

wingspan: A wingspan is the distance between the two tips of a bird's wings. A golden eagle's wingspan can be more than 7 feet (2 m) long.

INDEX

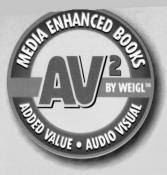

Log on to www.av2books.com

AV[2] by Weigl brings you media enhanced books that support active learning. Go to www.av2books.com, and enter the special code found on page 2 of this book. You will gain access to enriched and enhanced content that supplements and complements this book. Content includes video, audio, weblinks, quizzes, a slide show, and activities.

AV[2] Online Navigation

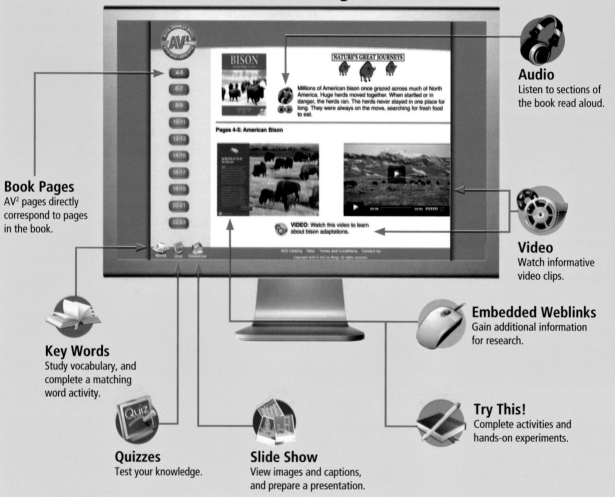

Book Pages
AV[2] pages directly correspond to pages in the book.

Key Words
Study vocabulary, and complete a matching word activity.

Quizzes
Test your knowledge.

Slide Show
View images and captions, and prepare a presentation.

Audio
Listen to sections of the book read aloud.

Video
Watch informative video clips.

Embedded Weblinks
Gain additional information for research.

Try This!
Complete activities and hands-on experiments.

AV[2] was built to bridge the gap between print and digital. We encourage you to tell us what you like and what you want to see in the future.

Sign up to be an AV[2] Ambassador at www.av2books.com/ambassador.